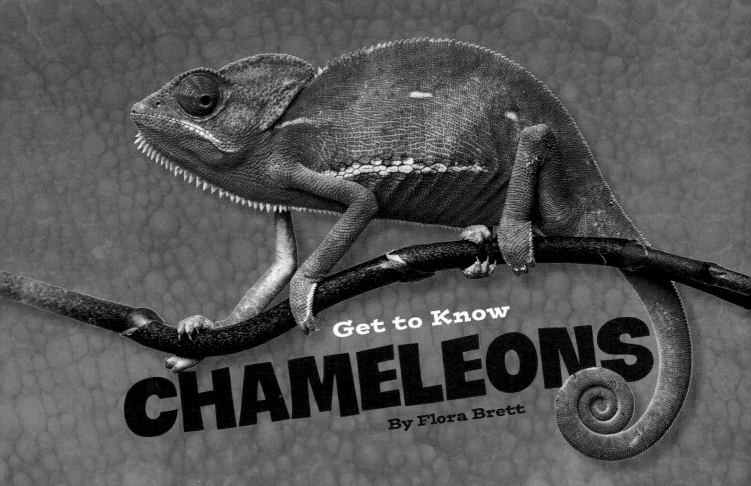

Get to Know
CHAMELEONS
By Flora Brett

CAPSTONE PRESS
a capstone imprint

First Facts are published by Capstone Press,
1710 Roe Crest Drive, North Mankato, Minnesota 56003
www.capstonepub.com

Library of Congress Cataloging-in-Publication Data
Brett, Flora, author.
Get to know chameleons / by Flora Brett.
        pages cm.—(First facts. Get to know reptiles)
Summary: "Discusses chameleons, including their physical features, habitat, range, diet, and life
cycle."—Provided by publisher.
Audience: Ages 6–9.
Audience: K to grade 3.
Includes bibliographical references and index.
ISBN 978-1-4914-2059-1 (library binding)
ISBN 978-1-4914-2243-4 (paperback)
ISBN 978-1-4914-2265-6 (ebook PDF)
1. Chameleons—Juvenile literature. I. Title.
QL666.L23B74 2015
597.95'6—dc23
                              2014023856

Editorial Credits
Nikki Bruno Clapper, editor; Cynthia Akiyoshi, designer;
    Svetlana Zhurkin, media researcher; Katy LaVigne, production specialist

Photo Credits
Dreamstime: Sigge, 19; Newscom: Photoshot/NHPA/Anthony Bannister, 15 (bottom); Shutterstock:
bluedogroom, 17, Cathy Keifer, 13, Claudia Naerdemann, 5, FikMik, 7, Ian Schofield (background), cover and
throughout, Kuttelvaserova Stuchelova, cover, 1, 24, MattiaATH, back cover, 21, Pierre-Yves Babelon, 11,
Ryan M. Bolton, 20; Wikipedia: Muhammad, 9

Printed in the United States of America in North Mankato, Minnesota.
092014   008482CGS15

Table of Contents

Colorful Communicators 4

Tails and Scales 6

Where Chameleons Live 8

Hidden Habitats 10

Dinnertime 12

Producing Young 14

Growing Up 16

Dangers to Chameleons 18

Protecting Chameleons 20

Amazing but True! 21

Glossary 22

Read More 23

Internet Sites 23

Critical Thinking Using the Common Core 23

Index 24

Colorful Communicators

Imagine being able to change the color of your skin in an instant. Chameleons have this amazing ability. These **reptiles** from the lizard family change colors to show mood. When a chameleon is frightened, its whole body changes color.

Like all reptiles, chameleons are **cold-blooded**. They need to keep their bodies warm. Temperature, light, and **humidity** all affect a chameleon's colors.

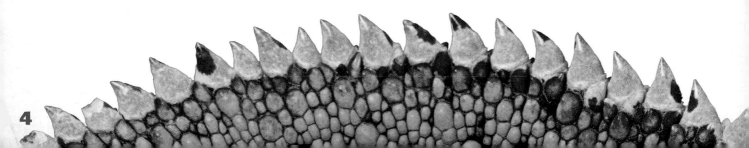

panther chameleon

Fact:
Chameleons vary in size.
The smallest are about 1 inch
(2.5 centimeters) long. The largest
are about 2 feet (0.6 meter) long.

reptile—a cold-blooded animal that breathes air and
has a backbone; most reptiles have scales

cold-blooded—having a body temperature that
changes with the surrounding temperature

humidity—the measure of the moisture in the air

Tails and Scales

A chameleon's body is made for living in trees. A chameleon grabs branches with its long tail and **pincers** on its feet.

Chameleons are normally green, gray, or brown. These colors blend in with trees and protect chameleons from **predators**.

Chameleons are covered with **scales**. Underneath the scales are four layers of different-colored skin cells. These cells change size when a chameleon changes color. The chameleon turns the color of the largest cells.

Fact:
A chameleon's tail helps the lizard balance in high winds.

green chameleon

pincer

pincer—a body part used to grasp and hold objects

predator—an animal that hunts other animals for food

scale—one of many small, hard pieces of skin that cover an animal's body

Where Chameleons Live

Most chameleons live on the African island of Madagascar. Some live on Africa's mainland and in southern Asia and Europe.

Many chameleons also live in Hawaii. In the 1970s people brought chameleons to Hawaii as pets. Many were let go in the wild. There were few predators to eat them, so the chameleons quickly spread.

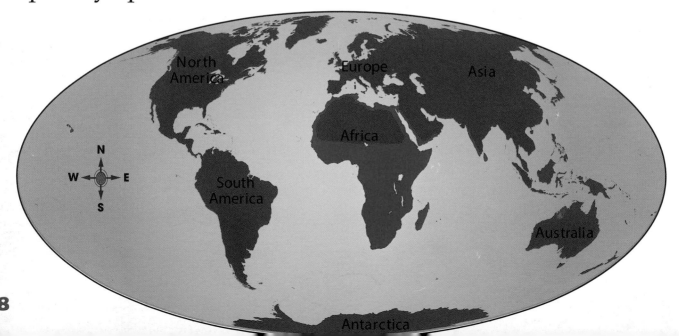

Fact:

Male Jackson's chameleons have horns. They use their horns to fight for territory.

Jackson's chameleon

Hidden Habitats

Chameleons live in many **habitats**. Most chameleons live in warm, wet **rain forests**. Others make their homes in hot, dry deserts. A few even live high in the mountains.

Chameleons spend most of their lives in trees. They are good climbers. Most chameleons don't spend much time on the ground. These slow movers are easy **prey** down there.

Fact:
Chameleons move less than 20 feet (6 meters) per minute on the ground.

habitat—the natural place and conditions in which an animal or plant lives

rain forest—a thick forest where rain falls nearly every day

prey—an animal hunted by another animal for food

11

Dinnertime

Chameleons spend most of their time hunting. They eat insects such as locusts, grasshoppers, and crickets. The tip of a chameleon's tongue is a ball of muscle. Like a sticky suction cup, it snatches prey.

Chameleons' bodies move slowly, but their tongues move fast! A chameleon can stick out its tongue at 13 miles (21 kilometers) per hour. A fast tongue is good for grabbing food.

Fact:

Chameleons can move their eyes in two different directions at the same time. This ability helps them spot prey.

veiled chameleon catching a fly

Producing Young

Chameleons change colors to **mate**. A female's pale colors let the male know he is allowed to come near.

Most female chameleons lay eggs in nests in the ground. A female may lay up to 100 eggs. She covers the **clutch** with dirt to hide it from predators.

A few types of chameleons have live young instead of laying eggs. These females give birth on tree branches.

mate—to join with another to produce young

clutch—a group of eggs laid at one time

Chameleon Life Cycle

A chameleon hatches and becomes an adult. Then it mates and has its own babies.

flap-necked chameleon digging a burrow for her eggs

Growing Up

After several months, the eggs are ready to hatch. **Hatchlings** leave the nest as soon as they are born. Baby chameleons know how to take care of themselves. They can hunt insects right away.

Chameleons grow quickly. Most **species** reach adulthood by age 2. Scientists do not know how long chameleons live in the wild.

hatchling—a young animal that has just come out of its egg

species—a group of animals with similar features

Dangers to Chameleons

Chameleons can't change their colors to blend in with surroundings. Hawks, owls, and other birds easily spot and eat chameleons.

People are also a threat to chameleons. Many people keep chameleons as pets. But caring for these lizards is hard. Many chameleons die quickly in **captivity**. Many countries limit the number of chameleons that can be **exported**. But illegal trade is still a problem.

captivity—an environment that is not a natural habitat

export—to send and sell goods to other countries

a southern ground hornbill carrying a chameleon

Fact:
Chameleons have the poorest hearing of all lizards. Their poor hearing can keep them from hearing predators nearby.

Protecting Chameleons

Some countries have created parks to protect chameleons. Several groups continue to check chameleon populations. A few species of chameleons are endangered. They might soon be gone forever. By protecting them, we can help all of these colorful lizards survive.

endangered rhinoceros chameleon

Amazing but True!

The large veiled chameleon lives in the dry mountains of Yemen and Saudi Arabia. This chameleon has a special water-collecting growth on its head called a casque. At night drops of moisture roll down the casque and into the chameleon's mouth. An adult's casque is about 2 inches (5 cm) long.

casque

Fact:

The veiled chameleon sometimes eats leaves to get extra water.

Glossary

captivity (kap-TIH-vuh-tee)—an environment that is not a natural habitat

clutch (KLUHCH)—a group of eggs laid at one time

cold-blooded (KOHLD-BLUHD-id)—having a body temperature that changes with the surrounding temperature

export (EK-sport)—to send and sell goods to other countries

habitat (HAB-uh-tat)—the place and natural conditions where an animal or plant lives

hatchling (HACH-ling)—a young animal that has just come out of its egg

humidity (hyoo-MIH-du-tee)—the measure of the moisture in the air

mate (MAYT)—to join with another to produce young

pincer (PIN-sur)—a body part used to grasp and hold objects

predator (PRED-uh-tur)—an animal that hunts other animals for food

prey (PRAY)—an animal hunted by another animal for food

rain forest (RAYN FOR-ist)—a thick forest where rain falls nearly every day

reptile (REP-tile)—a cold-blooded animal that breathes air and has a backbone; most reptiles have scales

scale (SKALE)—one of many small, hard pieces of skin that cover an animal's body

species (SPEE-sheez)—a group of animals with similar features

Read More

Connors, Kathleen. *Chameleons*. Really Wild Reptiles. New York: Gareth Stevens Pub., 2013.

Lawrence, Ellen. *A Chameleon's Life*. Animal Diaries: Life Cycles. New York: Bearport, 2012.

Petrie, Kristin. *Chameleons*. Minneapolis: ABDO Pub. Company, 2013.

Internet Sites

FactHound offers a safe, fun way to find Internet sites related to this book. All of the sites on FactHound have been researched by our staff.

Here's all you do:
Visit *www.facthound.com*
Type in this code: 9781491420591

 **Super-cool stuff!** Check out projects, games and lots more at **www.capstonekids.com**

Critical Thinking Using the Common Core

1. Chameleons change colors for different reasons. Explain three reasons why a chameleon would change colors. (Key Ideas and Details)

2. Think about how your body parts help you do different jobs. What parts of a chameleon's body help it survive? How? (Integration of Knowledge and Ideas)

Index

appearance, 4, 6, 14, 18, 21

bodies, 4, 6, 12

captivity, 18

clutch, 14

cold-blooded, 4

colors, 4, 6, 14, 18

dangers, 6, 10, 14, 18, 19, 20

eating, 12, 18, 21

eggs, 14, 16

eyes, 12

food, 12, 21

habitats, 10, 21

hatchlings, 15, 16, 17

hunting, 12, 16

live birth, 14

mating, 14, 15

nests, 14, 16

people, 8, 18, 20

pets, 8, 18

pincers, 6

predators, 6, 8, 14, 18, 19

prey, 10, 12

rain forests, 10

range, 8

reptiles, 4

scales, 6

size, 5, 16, 17, 21

species, 16, 20

tails, 6

tongues, 12

young, 14, 15, 16, 17